# Footprints of a Stranger

Also by Barbara Gurney and published by Ginninderra Press
*Life's Shadows*

Barbara Gurney

# Footprints of a Stranger

*Footprints of a Stranger*
ISBN 978 1 74027 767 9
Copyright © text Barbara Gurney 2012

First published 2012
Reprinted 2015

**GINNINDERRA PRESS**
PO Box 3461 Port Adelaide SA 5015
www.ginninderrapress.com.au

I've come this way with open heart
With tales of days well travelled

Reflect upon the unknown spirit
Explore the path together

# Contents

| | |
|---|---:|
| Footprints of a Stranger | 3 |
| Lamentation | 9 |
| The sigh that reaches us all | 10 |
| Loss | 11 |
| Legacy of the Land | 12 |
| The Dark Side of Nature | 13 |
| I shouldn't go there | 14 |
| Someone in Heaven | 15 |
| Carmen's Invitation | 17 |
| Secret Path | 18 |
| The Golden Bauble | 19 |
| Wastage of Warriors | 21 |
| Bulbs | 22 |
| Perchance to Love | 23 |
| Texture | 24 |
| Envy | 25 |
| Commitment | 26 |
| Smugglers | 27 |
| The Outstretched Hand | 28 |
| memory of depression | 29 |
| Somewhere between falling in love… | 29 |
| The Absence of a Rainbow | 31 |
| The Empty Chair | 32 |
| Offerings | 33 |
| Inside the Cover | 34 |
| Desecration | 36 |
| You | 37 |
| Shrouded Reality | 38 |
| Imperfection | 39 |
| Façade | 40 |
| The Miscarriage | 42 |

| | |
|---|---:|
| For Aubrey | 43 |
| I Gave My Heart | 45 |
| Morning Tea | 46 |
| The Candle of Life | 47 |
| My Child | 48 |
| Looking up, Looking down | 49 |
| Technofriend | 50 |
| The Immigrant | 51 |
| Today | 52 |
| In the Pursuit of Happiness | 53 |
| The Passing of Time | 55 |
| Touch My Hand | 56 |
| The Winter Witch | 57 |
| A Garden That Once Was | 58 |
| End of the Day | 60 |

# Lamentation

There's tomorrow to traverse
    from a day that clings
    cocooning the hurt
    afraid of release

Wandering the hours
    in search of a rainbow
    a starburst of shining
    potential of joy

Prepare a new path
    softly like a whisper
    let the pain fall from my heart
    slowly so I'll remember

# The sigh that reaches us all

The whale sighs
It breathes in pain
The skin dries and begins to wither
Insignificant waters wash in and out
and man tempts beast to live

Buckets and shrouds are used
but vainly one may think
Urging, striving, while sunset descends
The struggle built on freedom dreams
One succumbs, and man is distraught
but one is saved and blessings fall
Humbled against the might
the beach has left a memory

# Loss

Hidden in the folds of skirts are dreams that cannot be
Favourite blue jeans
lie where they fell from her tender frame
I cannot touch what once were hers
Memories are tucked beneath cotton and rayon
The pockets still hold her spirit

Some days I stand quietly wishing for her presence
A soft kiss
A gentle touch
Just one more precious moment
I hear my breath short with anguish
My palms face upwards as I ask, 'For what?'

The dust builds over teenage clutter
Emptiness pervades her space
I close my eyes
Concealing the view of the pillow
Dented where innocence slept
I must forsake her room

A life not fully used
Taken in a moment of steel upon steel
Shattering glass caused the sound of heartbreak
Claimed by senseless speed
Sirens announced pain
Then all went numb

When agony becomes acceptance
Her room may be my solace
Her face in the frame may laugh once more
The softness of her prettiest things may bring strength
Memories of shared joy may show me how to care again

# Legacy of the Land

Fences sag with age
barbed wire no longer a deterrent
the gate flaps with groans
but the mail box shines with fresh paint

Windmills creak around the rust
old pipes spew the water
into drums that had seen better days
it drips giving relief to grateful crawling beings

The tractor stands silent
dirt dried on wheels and places hidden
shovels and spades lean on the walls
worn by tasks completed for now

The farmer strides across open ground
brittle stubble crackles beneath boots tied with string
arms cursed like leather
from the days spent in the sun

The flies swarm around his brow
dust builds lines across the craggy face
sweat clogs the pores
while filling the eyebrows and overflowing

I pass on by and wonder
does love of the land grip the soul
of sons born of sons
into a heritage of country soil

# The Dark Side of Nature

She creeps between the grasses
Low and sleek
Eyes blink away the darkness as the hunt begins

She hurdles the obstacles
Swift and neat
The tip of her black tail flicks back and forth

She stalks her prey
Crouched and tense
Teeth hidden by the low light ready to kill

She accomplishes her goal
Fast and clean
Bones are exposed as claws rip into flesh

She devours her catch
Quick and complete
Blood spills from her jaw making rivers down her fur

She lies in soft sand
Content and relaxed
Stomach extended her body satisfied for now

I shouldn't go there

Where dreams turn to worthless images
    of shadows
        with monsters
            and dark evil thoughts

Creeping beasts of heartfelt longing
    of gloomy days
        with self-inflicted pain
            and obscure fantasies

My dark forbidden place
    of no tomorrow
        with despair
            and unending nothingness

But I do

# Someone in Heaven

A life has shrugged off its pain
left us behind
to mourn
to weep
while seeking to see the reason

This loved one
starts the journey to another place
where hurt is no longer
where misery flees
joy welcomes

Love extends beyond the ending
reaches out in absence
held close
to feel the belonging
of times past

Has my life been enough
to be remembered
when my time comes
have I spread happiness
been kind

Will I be rewarded
as this newly departed must be
will the gates of freedom
from anger
be shown to me

The unknown is pressing down
with heartache
I search
and take comfort in the knowledge
that I know someone in heaven

# Carmen's Invitation

Silken dress chosen from between the jeans
A face presented for reflected approval
Eager feet slip into heels and dance out the door
Expectation grasps the ticket

Ancient stones stand strong
Gathering anticipation from the street
Glittering interior clinks with champagne
The grandeur halted by common chatter

Fantasy builds as chimes announce culture
Seats fill, shoulders clash
Walls accept the emotion
A tasselled curtain wobbles to life

Trained voices clamour for receptive ears
Passion covers the sober stage
Colour explodes from swishing skirts
Velvet ascends from throats

The sounds of history are recorded
United applause surrounds success
Encore
Encore

Written with the memory of attending *Carmen* at the Prague Opera House

## Secret Path

The path to a happy life is the secret to be learned

Emotions of bliss can hide beneath the mundane
or be the cause of a smile when all alone
The pit of the stomach can be fluttering with beautiful
    butterflies
despite poverty or hardship pressing on the everyday
Laughter may not be the signpost of contentment
for the aura of a soul that's truly happy touches even strangers
Reputation, money and status should be the excesses of
    happiness
as the image of one's self reflects like a mirror into others' lives

Ponder on your moments of gladness
Hold tight the joyous memories
Hurry them into your future
Be aware of the true secret path

# The Golden Bauble

A golden bauble lies in my grasp
I hold it softly
for it could crush
into pieces
like my fragile heart

She accepted the birth of Christmas
and showed the joy of one redeemed
Her path was clear
Life trod easy on her soul

Caring for me
she ignored the expletives that filled my speech
My resolute distancing from faith
made her frown with sorrowful longing
that I would find her God

I delighted in knowing her
The connection was complete
We loved; despite our differences
Sharing earth's blessings
Becoming one

Bright flowers covered her coffin
and psalms were sung in praise
She wanted no mourning
for angels were waiting
welcoming the believer

The habit of Christmas faces me
Thoughts of celebration
Recollections build
The carols of The Child
The echoed hope for mankind

The bauble dangles freely
from a branch of my tree
It glistens
and cheers my heart
with memories

# Wastage of Warriors

Spinning, spinning, spinning
Flickering judgement
Pausing on torments; begging they be gone

Spinning
Reverberating horror
Visions of death spread around turncoat boots

Spinning
Enduring emotions
Wanting it somehow not to be true

Spinning
External control
Unmitigated fury at the wastage of warriors

Spinning
Tender sentiments
Pocketing sorrow without congealing the heart

Spinning
Duty commands
Stand to attention; advance on the mission ahead

On the killing of three Australian soldiers by a rogue Afghan soldier

# Bulbs

They urge through the soil
Compelled by nature
Bound for glorious colour
When their beauty is revealed

# Perchance to Love

My pillow is soft and comfortable and I luxuriate in the clean sheets and the warmth of my bed

Sleep evades me for the moment and I recall the day that has been
Did I do something to make myself proud?

It was an ordinary day really
Breakfast by the garden
The sun peaking above the fence
Silence from the neighbours while in the distance the traffic roared
I phoned a friend and listened to her worries

As I pull the covers under my chin, I consider myself blessed
My children are grown, managing their own lives with satisfaction
The bank balance dwindles but sustains me for a while
A home that is my own

I saw ragged men gathered by the river today
A cigarette being shared
They obviously had no other place to be
It made me wonder

The clock in the hall chimes half past eleven
I toss and turn
The aches of age creep between the sheets and I feel them own me
I frown although no one sees
Am I the person I should be?

## Texture

The colours blend
No end to their form

Flashes of yellow becoming jealous rage
A stage of my life I prefer to forget
Riches unreachable, stardom untouchable

Sorrow spotted on my biography
Like the geography of my feelings
Overshadowed but coloured into memories

Turn life around and option emerges
Surges with brightness, splatters and curses

Orange and pink clashing and vibrant
Bringing a sense of singing and dancing

Smudges and smears maketh the sum
Patterns and angles together are one

Look deep within patches of heartache
See what you make
See what you take

The colours blend
No end to their form

# Envy

It claws at the back of my eyes but I refuse to cry

It is not the creaseless faces
Or agile bodies that don't groan when bending
Nor the shared companionship
That creates this longing

Why is Praha so far?
Unable to be reached for a simple pleasure

I want to touch the top of the newborn head
To be the cause of that smile from behind the dummy
Tickle those toes
Cuddle the chubby body

I clutch my spoon and stir deliberately

Just a touch
a hug
a moment
I could be satisfied

# Commitment

Two men
One still a boy
Despite the number of birthdays
Seize the paddle
Battle the waves

The father
Watches with heart
Sees with his soul
Acknowledges the difficulties
But chooses the right path

The son
Learns and delights
With simple joy
Smiles readily at those around
While kindness ensures his pleasure

The teacher
Sees the bond that's unbroken
Between two men with one aim
Empathy touches his being
Kayaking is smooth water

# Smugglers

By darkened shore
Evil lurks
Content to let shadows hide the deeds
Hats pulled low
Over blackened faces
Eyes that dart
And feet that sneak
Nightfall covers mystery
And keeps their many secrets

# The Outstretched Hand

I feel…

>    like a piece of newspaper
>    clipped for its importance
>    discarded when the moment passes

Is society eager to outstretch its hand?
Not offering a touch of friendship
But grasping opportunity of self-benefit
Seeing others as a vessel of desires
Coveting that which isn't needed

Taking with gluttony and avarice?
I want
Must have

Has greed reduced us to begging without need?
Not seeing those whose hunger is real – barefooted and
    homeless
Is it Me first,
You only if excess is superfluous
Uncaring but for the bubble of self
Not sharing but for the joy of acquisition

The fires of society burn out of control
Scavenging
Looting
Because of the habit of using others

# memory of depression

i stood on the edge and looked down
to the depth
to the pit
beyond the crisp sharp bridge of time

i felt the clinging nothingness
the despair
the longing
when i sat in space that wasn't owned

i became covered with soiled pretence
no truth
no soul
only a tormented sigh of unwanted solitude

i cried out to be needed without necessity
for purpose
for function
to benefit no one except to share in the day

i wanted love without fraudulent emotions
without giving in
without giving up
when treason didn't surround peace

i looked up and love reflected
a caring touch
a heartfelt word
and the strength to begin again
Somewhere between falling in love…

      touching hands
      sparkling eyes
      mutual goals
      resolute attachment
      intermingling passion

and today,

      loud silences
      incumbent days
      clashing words
      wretched belonging
      diverse ambition

our hearts became lost

# The Absence of a Rainbow

What if the rainbow colours
Refused to join in the promise
When the rain was caressed by gentle light

The blue would fill a river
Splash between the reeds
Orange would bounce off sun's rays
The colour drunk in by the glow
Twirls of glee would see indigo dance
Peaking between thunder clouds
Dodging the lightening that encased the yellow
Fields of wind-blown young crops beckons
A ribbon of creeping green
Pretty heads of pansies
Curtsy with velvet skirts
Enfolded by violet sparkles straight from the sky

Each colour brings expansion in its own way
Nature would oblige
But the joy of that glorious vision
That spans the earth
That brings forth a gasp of beauty
Must be

Red, yellow starts the arc
With orange, green and blue
Bound alongside indigo and violet
For mere mortals eyes
The oath of a god that shows magnificence
Filling a dewy horizon
In the wonderful refraction
Of a rainbow

# The Empty Chair

Of decorated trees with shiny baubles
Or cradles in a manger
Christmas comes around each year
To families and to strangers

Joyous scenes may fill the day
And sadness can be broken
As Christmas comes around each year
With happiness sometimes a token

Each one feels and some will share
A difference in their heart
But Christmas comes around each year
To those held close, to those apart

There dwells within at Yuletide
To each we try to care
But Christmas comes around each year
And still the empty chair

# Offerings

Amid dust
and mud
Without shelter
and food

There was fear
and horror
There was loss, of life
and hope

They showed courage
and bravery
Although young
and raw

It brought freedom
and choice
Secured our future
and prospects

To show gratitude
and admiration
Some way to give back
and honour

Only my footsteps
on bitumen
And fingers
bringing music

I'm a grateful Australian who, as a member a pipe band, has played in Anzac Day parades for fifty years.

# Inside the Cover

Strong strides batter the footpath
The sun strikes the leather jacket
Tossed over the shoulder
Jeans torn by design hide expense
Tattoos exhibited on the swinging arm
Shout defiance of power
Resistance
Conflict

Patrons filling the morning in vacuity
Lift their gaze from ritual coffee
Pedestrians step aside
Stare
Condemn

Raven hair spiked for significant effect
Coloured with accented purple and blue
A curl of gold grips the nostril
Hands reposition the sunglasses
He glares at cars baring the way
Actions deemed a witness of aggression
Hostility
Violence

Coffee cups clatter
Eyebrows rise in common censure
Thoughts are almost audible
Blight on society
Weird

His eyes fall on a duo of childhood
Their puppy tangled at small feet
Myriad of earrings jangle as he stoops
Fingers adorned with metal
Quickly untangle the knots
The stud below his lip dances
He smiles
Eyes light up

He bows to the little ladies
And continues on his way

# Desecration

I doze
A vision comes to me

I am floating on a stagnant river
Murky scum surrounds me
My languid body is encumbered by debris
Pieces of weed catch on my toes
I let them stay there

No noise penetrates nature's sounds
But the wetness trickles into my ears
A slight tip of the head brings a splash to my lips
The taste is of discarded needs
Of waste and greed

The abhorrent litter circles me in unwanted attention
My agitated arms push at the litter
Feet kick at society's surplus
I become trapped in the reeds
My body is covered in oils of desecration

Unnourished leaves fall from the trees
Dead fish stay bound in algae
The lifeless water remains
There is no beauty in the river
Destroyed, even in dreams

I wake
The vision remains with me

# You

The world spins out of control
Above our cover is depleted
While seas are humanly polluted
And grass struggles in the spreading deserts

One person can make a difference
Like a pebble's wash reaching the shore
It starts with an encompassing passion
And grows out of a sorrowful pain

Reach out, cast aside your doubts
Embrace the daunting challenge
Stand up, bring the world your courage
For you can show who you are

# Shrouded Reality

Mist clings to the canvas of reality
Muted greens are painted across the valley
Trees move gently, welcoming the morning air
Creating minuscule transparent windows
Footsteps cross the crisp foreground

The distance reveals hills of grey
Hidden for a moment by the blinking eye
A dove huddles into its feathers
Magpies tiptoe leaving their futile mark
And sheep belong to each other

Cold air succumbs to the rising sun
Promising a day without chill
Soft amber and gentle blue spreads onto the palette
An easel stands expectantly
Eager to create a memory

# Imperfection

Damn it!
Perfection is a burden

Expectations are heavy

Excellence is forced on me
I cringe with unworthiness
My soul becomes shattered
Broken from trying

Surely
Character builds through flaws

Why shouldn't I be me
Without the pain of judgement

# Façade

Beside the walls of lies
    we glimpse back to the past
With insight of a world that was
    of tales that we've been told

The street is held in frozen disguise
    with gas lamps lit with mocking
The cobblestones under tourists' feet
    stand proud to be discovered

The endurance of every battered tool
    falls on the modern eye
Withstanding all that's handed out
    by stamina that survived

Faded labels tell of bygone trade
    loudly we point and stare
Glimpses of the way things were
    create memories of our own

We walk the path of history
    and memories are given credence
For in this street of pretence
    we wander for just a while

Not one doorway can be entered
    each shop bell will never ring
The joy of being in times of yore
    bring smiles from the wistful few

Heed the very commonness
    of what sits amongst the dust
For history is the passing of time
    in which we all belong

Written after a visit to the Transport Museum in Glasgow, where a street of a bygone era has been reconstructed

# The Miscarriage

We lost her
You know
Just a pea shape
Not yet a child
Hopes and dreams were forming
As she lay in the womb
Becoming part of our family
Snuggling into hearts
But now
Only a diamond in our memory

# For Aubrey

The mud sat
Day after day
Refreshed into an unyielding enemy by tropical rain

Continuous rice and bully beef
Hid hunger but provided no comfort
Fear sat alongside cold tea
While rustling grasses kept ears alert

Blisters formed from socks that bit
Stomachs gripped until they yielded
Each sodden path challenged the spirit
Night brought no relief

The sky was a place too close
Splattered by jungle green
Squadrons came and spilt their fury
While tracers leapt from grounded guns

When combat shook life
The mud pebbled with youthful blood
Trodden with desperate boots
Lest injured mates be left in drowning squelch

Arms enfolded lingering lives
Tears fell for what might have been
With tribute each comrade was remembered
Anger filled minds as aim was taken

Always one more mile
The dread of advancing enemy
Expectation of a covert death
Quietness no less daunting than a melee of shouting foe

Far-off places where loved ones waited
Dreams of warmth long lost
Only men with similar pains
Broke the solitary thoughts each soldier held

The mud sat
Day after day
Many men fell while knee deep in its grip

For my father Aubrey Cecil Hannah, who fought in New Guinea in World War II

# I Gave My Heart

I'm touched by a demanding hand
Then tossed aside with gratuitous neglect
Humility, abandonment expected
Without love the evening ends

Perched on the edge of our bed
My beauty buried by scorn
Scoffed at for no reason
His contempt swallowing my joy

Feelings trampled with disregard
I'm left alone to wonder why
Sitting scrunched up with sorrow
My confidence assaulted – injured

Yesterdays are mocked for effect
I cringe as I'm teased
Tears only bring resentment
I'm derided for having a care

Why do my emotions go unheeded?
What justifies this conflict?
Will my love be returned?
How did it end like this?

I expected the best
In a life that was to be forever
But I sit by myself and ponder
Was I wrong when I gave my heart?

# Morning Tea

Noise of continuing business
A hint of music
The whirring of unrequired fans
The brisk winter outside shows voices
Clink, clink of stirring spoons
Aroma of a long black
Sticky joy of chosen delights
Moments stolen from an ordinary life

# The Candle of Life

Flickering against sources not seen
Bending softly with puffs of pain
Shuddering with panic
Amid struggles
Caused by surrounding turmoil

Burnt into recall
Scorched by lessons of torment
Scars when touched
Convey memories
Intense once more

A flame of hope
Dancing with colours blended in pleasure
Expressing glimmering delight
Melting the hardest core
Sharing the arc of its heat

Yield gently
Reflect sincerely
Impart joyfully

# My Child

For my child I wish an open heart

Sadness and grief
Touches the soul
Gladness
Radiates through joy

The world draws in
Yet boundless be
Learn
Experience to gain

Feelings to treasure
Born of endurance
Encloses
Love is a promise

For my child I have hope

# Looking up, Looking down

Feet step in the rhythm of misery
The world enfolds the loneliness
Bringing no sight to more than oneself
As solitary thoughts continue to grind

With eyes down, the heart droops
Shoulders sag, and people pass by
Introspection bears no gain
And despondence overwhelms the soul

The world brings joy from a smile
Flowers peek out of a welcoming earth
Traffic spills people with places to go
Greeting friends, sharing stories with heart

Heads that are lifted show twinkling eyes
Gracing the day with enthusiasm on show
Touching each within the shared space
Bringing echoes of gladness into the day

# Technofriend

Treading the quickest path
Between waking and our rest
Unscheduled marvels are snubbed in haste

Morning dew falls on unseen beauty
A newborn rose ruptures without applause
Unheeded because of the sweeping hand heralded to be obeyed
As the air softens into glorious evening
We hurry to view someone else's dream

A loved one welcomed only in keystrokes
Friendship touted by technology
We care without a voice

# The Immigrant

Wrapped in a cocoon of unknown words
My day is full of silence
I ache, I long for friendship
But chance eludes the moment
When I can not interpret

Tradition commands attention
Even in one's chosen land
The old, the new
Stand confused in mind
While the heart desires belonging

I stand at a distance from others
Deaf to what is said
Mute, language poor
Few around speak my tongue
And I remain a stranger

I ask for your understanding
As familiar joys are gone
Shatter my cocoon
Bid my fears farewell
Welcome me with caring

# Today

Today I sit alone in pain
Apart from the busy world

Absorb the sounds of my beating heart
Watch my chest move in and out

I haven't combed my hair
My dressing gown has added crumbs

Shoulders beg towards the ground
My chin on an ageing breast

Curtains keep the shining out
But a knocking interrupts

A walking cane bears the weight of me
Slippers drag on dirty floors

Startled by the glare of company
My painted smile appears

# In the Pursuit of Happiness

A child skips
Feet lifting with joy
Giggles of school girls
Over nonsense shared
Youth reflects happiness
With ease

An old man whistles
Tunes spring from his past
Visits from friends
Phone calls ring blessings
His day ends complete

A new baby
Brings a glow
Wrapping memories into the heart
Renewing promises of love
Which echo down time

Cats purr satisfaction
Curled on one's lap
Softness of fur
Touches more than the hand
A ball or a stick
A tail shows delight
Companionship
Loyalty gained
Loneliness lost

Smiles given to strangers
Helps both passers-by
Spontaneous laughter
Bids all be a part
Contagious exhilaration
Glee leaps to the face

Anticipation of pleasure
Makes time disappear
Bliss enters the mind
Of delights still to come

Small actions
Cause ripples
The old remedy proven
Medicine of the soul
In the pursuit of happiness

# The Passing of Time

He knew when work was tough
And sweat leapt from every pore
Of hardships
Of empty pockets
Of unrequited dreams

He knew the joy of willing neighbours
The friendship of a beer shared
The soft glow of home-shed light
A family
And welcoming arms

He knew the many forms of love
A romance
A smile
A tail that wagged
A garden that grew

Now he sees that all has passed
Memories are a haven
Tired body moves little
Love is gone
Days pass

The old man cries

# Touch My Hand

Touch my hand
Let it linger with intention
A glance, a smile, pass it on to me
Make the journey to love

Silence is never golden when hearts are out of tune

Touch my hand
Impart your depth of feeling
A glance, a smile, pass it on to me
Make today the centre of our love

Absence never builds fondness when thoughts are someplace
    else

Touch my hand
Plan for joy and tender passion
A glance, a smile, pass it on to me
Make me believe in love

The world never turns if love does not enfold

Touch my hand
Bring me closer to the truth
A glance, a smile, pass it onto me
Make a promise for love

# The Winter Witch

Winter throws a seasonal tantrum
Rain floods on soggy soil
Wind shudders across tender leaves
Anger vents with thundering clashes

Rain floods on soggy soil
Dancing hail yields icy tears
Anger vents with thundering clashes
Skyline exposed by shards of light

Dancing hail yields icy tears
Trees submit beneath the clouds
Skyline exposed by shards of light
The storm intensifies with wrath

Trees submit beneath the clouds
Wind shudders across tender leaves
The storm intensifies with wrath
Winter throws a seasonal tantrum

# A Garden That Once Was

I sit
Unmoveable
I see the weeds that have grown quickly through the soil,
    reaching up towards the blueness
Puffs of dainty seeds are ready to increase the invasion
The chosen plants struggle
I long to grip the hose and bring relief to the begging soil
It is not possible

I look at the dry heads that once were dancing daffodils
Without intervention, they soaked up the rain and sent a
    burst of colour to please my eye
Then yielding, withered and died

Petunias no longer show their glory
They lay hidden, shrivelled beneath the mess of tangled grass

Labour can't be enjoyed and nature shows her strength
I turn the wheels of my confinement and shed a tear
Broad expanse of lawn no longer exists
Only flowers not wanted, and grass heads that flap in the
    breeze

I remember days of joy
Digging and planting with hope of new seasons
A peep of colour now defies the brittle stems
They too are weeds, but nature has no distinction
Dandelions bounce with colourful determination
And the bees work at the miracle that starts right here
I reach out
Nothing welcome can be touched

The weeds bend beneath my wheels
I see where I've been and am not displeased by the
 destruction
With thistles weaving through the thorns, the rose stands
 defiant
Spreading perfume of delight, and showing a spirit of which
 I'm proud
It is a pleasant moment
I savour it

I know my best was done when vigour and youth abounded
But now I have only memories
Of a garden that once was

# End of the Day

The day lengthens into dusk
Headlights make an endless trail
I end my toil

A warm glow beckons from the window
The key releases the welcome
And I am home

www.ingramcontent.com/pod-product-compliance
Lightning Source LLC
Chambersburg PA
CBHW070051120526
44589CB00034B/1910